The
Wild Witches'
Journal

A book for dreams, schemes and the weaving of words.

With love and thanks to my Spirit Guide, Nasawi, who encouraged, supported and aided the creating of this book and who never ceases to remind me that wisdom and happiness already spark within us, if we just take the time to find them.

Contents....

My Journal page contents...

This book I scribe with secret deeds.
To bring so forth my earthly needs.

No other eyes to peer or pry.
No other nose to seek or spy.

Weaving thoughts and words I spin.
Bless this book and all within.

The Wheel of the Year

Yule
Winter Solstice
N.H. 20th - 23rd Dec
S.H. 21st - 22nd Jun

N.H = Northern Hemisphere

S.H = Southern Hemisphere

Samhain
N.H. 31st Oct - 1st Nov
S.H. 30th Apr - 1st May

Imbolc
N.H. 2nd Feb
S.H. 1st Aug

Mabon
N.H. 21st - 24th Sep
S.H. 21st Mar

Ostara
N.H. 19th - 22nd Mar
S.H. 21st - 23rd Sep

Lughnasadh
Lammas
N.H. 1st Aug
S.H. 2nd Feb

Litha
Summer Solstice
N.H. 19th - 23rd June
S.H. 21st 22nd Dec

Beltane
N.H. 1st May
S.H. 31st Oct - 1st Nov

YULE
PLANNER

Festivities and Events

Recipes and Spells

Altar Plan

IMBOLC PLANNER

Festivities and Events

Recipes and Spells

Altar Plan

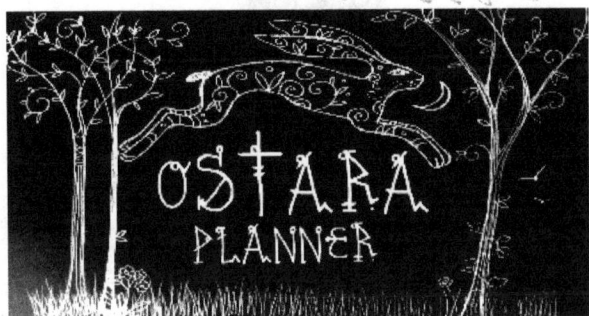

OSTARA PLANNER

Festivities and Events

Recipes and Spells

Altar Plan

BELTANE PLANNER

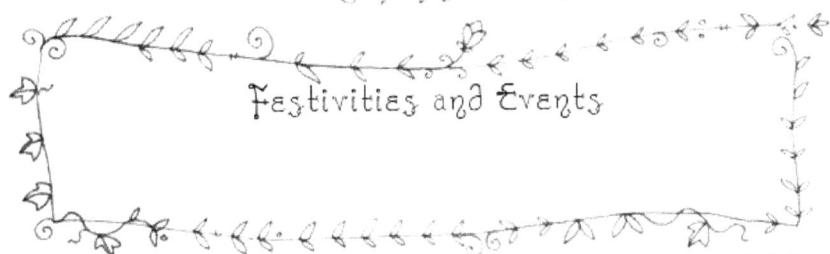

Festivities and Events

Recipes and Spells

Altar Plan

LITHA
PLANNER

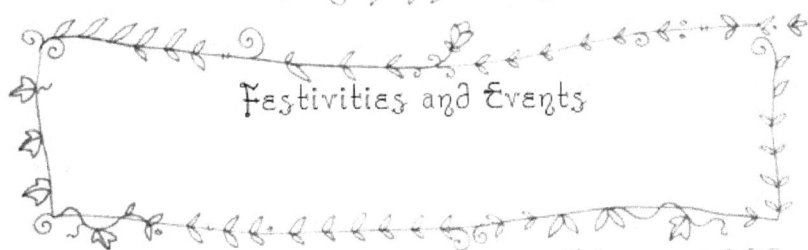

Festivities and Events

Recipes and Spells

Altar Plan

LUGHNASADH PLANNER

Festivities and Events

Recipes and Spells

Altar Plan

MABON
PLANNER

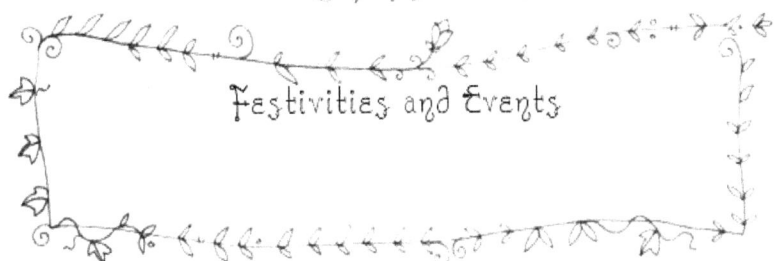

Festivities and Events

Recipes and Spells

Altar Plan

SAMHAIN PLANNER

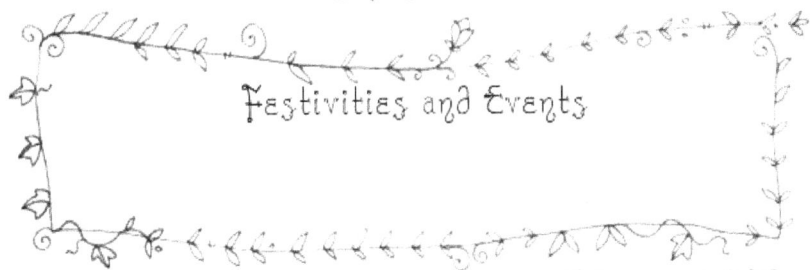

Festivities and Events

Recipes and Spells

Altar Plan

MOON PHASES

DARK MOON
Shadow Work
Ancestors
Rest

NEW MOON
Setting Goals
Abundance
Career

WAXING MOON
Love
Luck
Healing

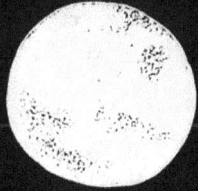

FULL MOON
Everything!
Insight
Divination

WANING MOON
Removing
Protection
Change

The Rabbit Meditation ~ Simplicity

I you ever feel too tired to carry all your worries and responsibilities, then take a few moments to sit with Rabbit. You will find him in a green meadow full of flowers, butterflies and bees....

You can see rabbit, in his meadow. His nose twitches and a dandelion leaf bobs up and down as he chews. His bright eye watches you sit beside him in the soft grass.

'Hello.' he says, turning to nibble at a yellow flower 'What's that on your back? It looks heavy.'

'It's a backpack full of rocks.' You answer. ' There's one for each of my responsibilities.'

Rabbit turns sideways to look at you again. He looks amused and slightly baffled. H as he thinks for a minute.

'You must be very fond of your responsibilities to want so many. The only thing I want on my back is the afternoon sun.'

Rabbit hops over and peers into the backpack. He makes a low whistle..' So many rocks! Do you really need all that?

Slowly you take all the rocks from your backpack and you recognise each worry and care that they represent. Then, with careful thought, you discard the ones you no longer need. You stack them into a cairn and put back into your backpack only the rocks that you do need.

Rabbit takes little notice. He is busy chewing and dreaming, but you feel lighter now and wonder why you carried so much with you all this time.

Like Rabbit, you can now feel the sun on your back and know that life only becomes cluttered and complicated if you allow it to.

As you turn to go home again you hear the voice of Rabbit. He reminds you...

'You have a choice. You always have a choice.'

Choices

Things I need to carry...

Things I don't need to carry...

Run free..

Time to
DREAM...

Speak ye here of dreams,
of sight...
and visions clear.....

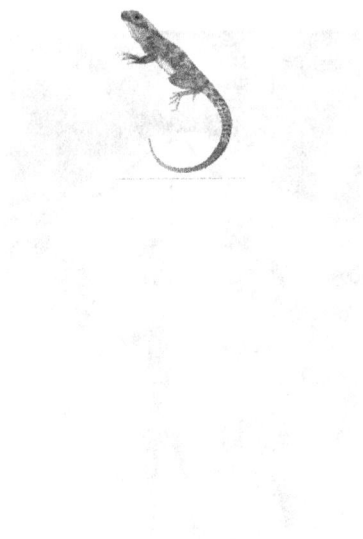

Speak ye here of what thou will .....

The Salmon ~ Perseverance

What flies but has no wings?
What heals but also stings?

TREE OF LIFE

See beyond sight...

The Spirit of the Forest...

Above my bed, one winter's night
A tiny soul within a light...

BLESS MY HOME

We are all connected ...all as one....

The Woodpecker ~ Communication & Resourcefulness

What is your Heart's Desire?...

At the bottom of my garden was a tiny wee man....

And above and around flew the Guardians of the Stones...

Sometimes it's just best to let it go...

We are the Seekers of Truth.

A chaos of brambles and trees
in the watering sun and the secretive breeze....

Some days the only sense comes from those who don't talk.

Let your thoughts fly....

Pumpkins and Snails... There's no great hurry....

Life is a twist of tangles

Bramble – Oghman Name: Muin
Healing . Protection. Abundance.

Bramble Harvest

Far, far away...above the normal people and all their weird confusion.

Moongazers. Happy to see a familiar face.

Attraction....

Spaces left to breathe...

The Jay.
A flash of blue and buff.
A rare jewel amidst the leaves.

As Within So Without

A storm brewing...Hold tight. It will pass.

Always looks to the light.

Stretching the muscles of the mind...

Stop. ...Breathe. ..Focus.

Archangel Michael
Protection

Those who care will always wait...

Reflection...

Eternal Flame

About the Artist and Writer:

Rachael Revelle of 3Sisters Crafts trained as a painter and printmaker. Since then many moons have passed and she now enjoys creating stained glass art, poetry and prose, as well as painting and printing.

Rachael

She works closely with her Kaskaskian Spirit Guide, Nasawi, who is always inspiring and supportive of her work. Together they endeavour to send healing into the world through image, word and thought.

Nasawi

Contact Rachael or buy from her Etsy shop..

EMAIL......
rachael-3sisters@outlook.com

WEBSITE & ETSY SHOP...
x3sisterscrafts.patternbyetsy.com

·